Lost At Sea
The Adventures of Max & Mimi at Topsail Island

© Big Daddy Productions LLC
Cleveland, Ohio

LOST AT SEA
The Adventures of Max & Mimi At Topsail Island

Written by Deborah Wilcox
Illustrated by Bob Livengood

Dedicated to Dougie and Wil
"May the wind carry you to peace and tranquility"

Topsail Island

In the 1700's, pirates sailed the coastal waters of North Carolina from the Outer Banks to Cape Fear. With its sparsely populated coast, it was a favorite place for hiding and for hunting merchant ships. Topsail Island got its name from pirate ships that would anchor their vessels in the sound and wait for merchant ships to arrive. From the sea, only their topsails were visible, hence the name Topsail, (pronounced Tops'l).

Max rolled his eyes, strained all over, and decided to, maybe, get up. Then he went back to sleep.

"Perfectly normal," thought Mimi Sue. "He wakes up, looks around, and then goes back to sleep. Perfectly normal." She yawned and looked around. "I'll go down to the sound. See what's going on."

"Oh, what a beautiful Topsail day!" thought Mimi, "It's a shame Max is missing all this." She watched as the world woke up. "My goodness," she said, "I see flowers everywhere! And birds…..flying in the air! What a gorgeous day this will be!"

"Well, I guess I'd better get up. Shake a leg!" Max said.

"Rock 'n roll! Here I come!"

He went down the steps and ran over to Mimi. "What are we doing today? I feel really good today! Really good!"

"Shhhhhhhhhhh. I'm looking at the world. It's marvelous!" said Mimi.

"Oh boy! I guess I'd better find something else to do! Mimi, you're nuts!"

Max decided to run. And he did. He ran out to the Topsail sound and back… leaving cat tracks all around. Then he ran up a tree and slipped back down. Without pause, he ran all the way to the ocean. Then he stopped.

"Look at that!" Max thought as he admired the sun sparkling off the ocean. "Wow! What a world! I guess I'd better go tell Mimi!"

Mimi was watching. "I just love him so. For a black cat with white paws he's all right with me!"

Max and Mimi were lying on the porch when Maria, their mother, came out. "OK everybody, it's time for me to leave. Max, stay in the yard 'til I come home to Topsail. Mimi, I know you'll be here when I get back. Be sweet now, I'll be home early."

Max yawned and Mimi smiled. It was a good thing that Maria didn't know everything they did. Especially Max!

Mimi jumped in her rocking chair and fell fast asleep. It was time for a nap. Max was just about to join her when he saw a beautiful lizard sunning on the walk. "Look at the blue and yellow tail and those big feet!" thought Max. He slinked toward the lizard, but the lizard was fast as lightening!

"Where did he go?" said Max. "I was going to catch him and now he's gone!"

"Oh well," thought Max, "might as well take a walk. Just a short walk."

It was a wonderful Topsail day, just like Mimi had said. Max decided to see what was going on at the pier, then go back and rest with Mimi.

"I wonder where that boat is going?" thought Max. "I bet it's off to see the world!"

And then, Max smelled shrimp! His little feet carried him up the dock and there he was, on the boat!

"I sure hope we have a good day today," said the Captain of the boat. "Let's get going."

All of a sudden, Max didn't know what to do. He was on the boat and the boat was moving across the water!

"We'll make it offshore in less than an hour." said Captain Dawson. "The shrimp will be there, that's for sure."

Max skittered to safety under an old tarp. He needed time to think!

Mimi had a good nap. She jumped off the rocking chair and thought, "I wonder where Max is? Probably in the house. I'll go look." Mimi searched all over the house, but no Max.

"Oh, he's in the back of the house, chasing lizards no doubt. I'll go find him." But Max wasn't there either. Mimi started to worry.

"I know he's here somewhere. I'll look at the neighbor's house. He couldn't have gone far. I'll find him!"

But Max had vanished. Completely!

Mimi was out of her mind with worry! Where could Max be? She had looked under and over everything. She had checked the houses, everyone of them. No luck.

"Oh Maxie. You have to be somewhere! You can't just disappear!"

It was getting very late in the day. Maria would be home soon. Mimi thought how she was going to tell her.

It was a hard thing to do!

When Maria came home, Mimi was waiting at the top of the steps.

"Mimi, you look so sad. Where is Maxie? More than likely, he's out back looking for lizards. I'll go inside and change my clothes. And Mimi, you look for Max."

When Maria came outside again, with a cool glass of lemonade, Mimi climbed up into her lap.

"Oh Maria!" thought Mimi, "it's awful! I can't find Max!"

"Okay, okay. I'll go find Max! I know that's what you want." said Maria, as she stroked Mimi's head. She put the lemonade down and started down the steps.

Max huddled under the tarp as the boat headed out to sea. He was a little bit scared but he hoped no one would notice him.

The fishermen were catching shrimp. Big ones, little ones, all kinds. Suddenly a big fish flapped across the deck and slid under the tarp.

"Well, would you look at that!" the Captain cried. "It's Max! Come down to catch a fish, huh?"

Max knew the Captain. He had been at their house many times. Max looked up at the Captain. "Oh boy! I'm in a heap of trouble now." thought Max.

"We'll get you a box. That way you'll be safe while we shrimp. Maybe we'll have some snacks for you, too. And then when we get back to Topsail, I'll take you home."

Max smiled and started to purr. It was going to be all right!

Max was fine now. He sat in the box and watched everything the fishermen did. There were shrimp everywhere! "I miss Mimi a lot, wonder what she's up to? Just sleeping, I guess."

Max watched as the fishermen hauled in another batch. Then, all of a sudden, Max and the box were trapped in the net! The Captain laughed and said, "Max, you're a catfish now! Then he pulled the net off Max's box and Max jumped out.

"Excitement's over," said the Captain. "You can go back to sleep, Max."

"Yep, nap time," thought Max with a yawn, as he jumped back into his box and curled up to sleep.

Maria looked all over the island, with Mimi right behind her.

"Say, have you seen Max? We can't find him anywhere."

"No, but we'll keep an eye out for him. He'll turn up." everyone assured Maria and Mimi.

Then an old man came riding by on his bicycle.

"You know, this morning as I was riding my bike down by the pier, I thought I saw Max going over to Capt. Dawson's shrimp boat. Do you think he's gone shrimping?"

That was all Maria needed to hear. "Come on Mimi! We'll call the Coast Guard! They'll know what to do. If Max is out to sea, they'll find him!"

The seawater was beautiful. It sparkled like jewels. Then Max started to notice the wind. It was breezy and sort of cold. "I'll stay in my box. It's kind of cozy here," thought Max. The captain looked at the sky and said, "We're going to have a squall! Look at those clouds! And I hear thunder! Put the shrimp on ice! And move Max inside the deck!" The fisherman moved quickly to get ready for the storm. Suddenly Max was afraid. A fisherman grabbed him and he struggled to get free. The fisherman slipped and Max flew straight into the sea!

"Ma'am, you say you lost your cat on a shrimp boat? Out in the sea? That's highly unlikely Ma'am. Cats aren't fond of boats. At all!" said the Coast Guard officer in charge.

"Well I don't care, I have to find Max! I think he's out in the sea and I know he's scared!! Can you do something?"

Maria was frantic. So was Mimi.

"Okay, Ma'am, I'll tell the radio operator to put out an alert. We'll see if we can find him."

"Great!" said Maria. "Thank you very much!"

Maria hung up the phone and turned to Mimi. "Mimi, don't be afraid. Max is going to come home. You have to believe!"

But Mimi looked so sad.

Max hit the seawater with a huge splash! He came up for air and he could see lightning everywhere! Then he went down again.

The fisherman grabbed a lifebuoy and threw it to Max.

"Bull's eye!" said the Captain, "We've got him!"

Max was dead-centered in the lifebuoy. The fisherman reeled him in and Max dove under the tarp.

"He'll be all right. He's just scared." said the Captain. "Let's go home! This rain is bad for business!"

Max looked out from under the tarp. He was shaking all over, but he was okay.

"Just let me go home to Mimi and Maria!"

It was a brilliant Topsail sunset. Mimi watched the pink and gold colors as the sun slipped in the sky. She knew Max would like it. She could see him in her mind.

"Oh Mimi! Look at the colors! Isn't it grand?" That is what Max would say.

"Maybe he'll come back. Maria said he would. He must come back! We have so many things to do!" thought Mimi.

Just then the phone rang.

"Ma'am, this is Captain Marlowe with the Coast Guard. We've found out where Max is."

Maria sighed and smiled. "That's wonderful news! Where is he?"

"He's on Captain Dawson's shrimp boat. They should be coming around Topsail Island right about now. They had a big squall out there and they almost lost Max."

"Is he all right?" asked Maria anxiously.

"Oh, he's fine now. But I'll bet he can't wait to see dry land."

Max wanted to go home to Topsail.

Captain Dawson said, "We'll be there in just a minute. Hold your horses!"

"What does he mean by that?" thought Max. "Probably a fish thing."

"Hey Maxie, let's have some fun! You can wear this!" The Captain pulled out a handkerchief and put it around Max's head.

"Now you're a pirate! said the Captain. "What do you think about that?"

Max didn't care. All he wanted was to be in safe harbor. Then he saw Maria! And Mimi! He was jumping for joy!

    Mimi could see Max on the boat. "Hallelujah!" she thought. "I can see him right there!"

 "What in the world does he have on his head?", Maria asked. "Oh, I see, he's got a pirate's scarf on! That's just like our Max. Always styling!!"

    Mimi shook her head with almost laughter. "My Maxie." said Mimi sighing.

    They watched as the boat pulled into the dock.

The fishermen tied the boat off, but Max couldn't wait any longer! He came down off the bridge, jumped on to the deck and ran straight off the boat. Then he was off and running. Mimi was right behind him! Captain Dawson laughed out loud!

"Well, Max wanted to go fishing and he did. But we've had a time of it with that squall. Max was a trooper, though. When he went into the sea, he wouldn't give up."

Maria was smiling, "That's my Max."

   Mimi was watching as Max took a big drink of water. Then he had another.

   "Boy, this water is good stuff! Cold, refreshing!" said Max.

   "What about all the water in the sea?" asked Mimi.

   "Well," said Max, "the sea has salt in it. I could taste it when I started swimming. Mimi, you should have seen me swimming! I was good!"

   "I bet you were good, Maxie. Very good indeed. But you wouldn't go back in the sea again, would you, Max?"

   "Only in an emergency," said Max. "After all, I'm a pirate now!"

When Maria came up to the house, Max and Mimi were lying on the porch, as usual. Maria got the rocking chair, sat down and said, "What in the world, Maxie, were you thinking?"

"Oh boy, I'm in trouble again!" Mimi climbed into Maria's lap. She knew what to do. "Come on, Max, get in here with Mimi. Just look at your pirate's scarf!" "Well, I think it's neat. Don't you, Mimi?" Mimi just smiled and closed her eyes.

All was quiet on Topsail that night. The stars were spectacular. It was a full moon. Maria had gone to bed hours ago. Max and Mimi were sitting on the dock listening to the sounds of the night. "Oh, Maxie! Look at the sound and the sky! It's so beautiful." Max, who still had his scarf on, was watching a lizard who was also watching him from a piling. "I can do it," said Max. "Watch this"

www.ingramcontent.com/pod-product-compliance
Lightning Source LLC
Chambersburg PA
CBHW041538040426
42446CB00002B/148